Questions and Answers: Countries

Venezuela

A Question and Answer Book

by Karen Bush Gibson

Consultant:
Daniel Hellinger
Professor of Political Science
Webster University
St. Louis, Missouri

Capstone press
Mankato, Minnesota

Fact Finders is published by Capstone Press
151 Good Counsel Drive, P.O. Box 669, Mankato, Minnesota 56002.
www.capstonepress.com

Library of Congress Cataloging-in-Publication Data
Gibson, Karen Bush.
    Venezuela: a question and answer book / by Karen Bush Gibson; consultant, Daniel
    Hellinger.
    p. cm.—(Fact finders. Questions and answers. Countries)
    Summary: "Describes the geography, history, economy, and culture of Venezuela in a
question-and-answer format"—Provided by publisher.
    Includes bibliographical references and index.
    ISBN–13: 978–0–7368-6413–8 (hardcover)
    ISBN–10: 0–7368–6413–X (hardcover)
    1. Venezuela—Miscellanea—Juvenile literature. I. Title. II. Series.
F2308.5.G53 2007
987—dc22   2006005059

Editorial Credits
Silver Editions, editorial, design, and production; Kia Adams, set designer; Ortelius Design,
    Inc., cartographer; Jo Miller, photo researcher; Scott Thoms, photo editor

Photo Credits
AP/Wide World Photos/Fernando Llano, 19; Corbis, 20; Corbis/Jorge Silva, 8; Corbis/
Michael Freeman, 23; Corbis/Pablo Corral V, 21; Getty Images Inc./AFP/Juan Barreto,
9; Getty Images Inc./Photographer's Choice/Hisham Ibrahim, 11; Getty Images Inc./
Richar Rondon-El Tiempo, 12; Getty Images Inc./The Image Bank/Larry Dale Gordon,
27; Houserstock/Dave G. Houser, 25; Index Stock Imagery/HIRB, 17; One Mile Up,
Inc., 29 (flag); Photo Courtesy of Paul Baker, 29 (coins); Peter Arnold/WWI/David
Woodfall, 4; Peter Arnold/WWI/Mike Lane, 1; Photodisc, 16; Richard Sutherland, 29
(bill); Shutterstock/Felix Fernandez Gonzalez, 18; South American Pictures, 13, 15;
South American Pictures/Tony Morrison, cover (background); Victor Englebert, cover
(foreground); Wolfgang Kaehler, 7

Table of Contents

Features

Where is Venezuela?

Venezuela is a country in South America. It is more than twice as large as the U.S. state of California.

The snow-capped peaks of the Andes Mountains in northwestern Venezuela give way to the central plains, called *llanos*. Snow from the mountains feeds rivers in the llanos.

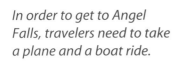

In order to get to Angel Falls, travelers need to take a plane and a boat ride.

Map of Venezuela

Legend
- ✪ Capital
- ● City
- ▲ Mountain Peak
- Mountain Range
- River
- = Waterfall

Caribbean Sea

TRINIDAD AND TOBAGO

Maracaibo

Barquisimeto

Caracas

Petare

Valencia

Lake Maracaibo

VENEZUELA

Tucupita

Ciudad Bolívar

Ciudad Guayana

Pico Bolívar

Andes Mountains

Apure River

Llanos

Orinoco River

Guayana Highlands

Caura River

Caroní River

Angel Falls

GUYANA

COLOMBIA

N
W E
S

Orinoco River

BRAZIL

Scale
0   100   200 Miles

0   100   200 Kilometers

Flat-topped mountains called *tupuys* are found in the Guayana Highlands of southwestern Venezuela. This is where Angel Falls, the highest waterfall in the world, plunges from a cliff.

When did Venezuela become a country?

Venezuela became a country in 1821. Before then, it was ruled by Spain.

Christopher Columbus claimed Venezuela for Spain soon after he arrived in 1498. Spain ruled the Venezuelans for more than 300 hundred years.

During the early 1800s, Venezuelans, led by Simón Bolívar, fought for their freedom from Spain. Spain lost the battle in 1821.

Fact!

When explorers arrived, they saw houses that reminded them of the Italian city of Venice. The explorers soon called this area "Little Venice" or Venezuela.

Sculptures and statues of Simón Bolívar can be found all over Venezuela.

Dictators ruled Venezuela for many years. Venezuelans **protested** against their lack of rights and say in the government. In 1958, the last dictator was overthrown.

What type of government does Venezuela have?

Venezuela's government is a **democracy**. Citizens can vote for their leaders when they are 18 years or older. Elections for the National Assembly are held every five years. This legislature makes laws for the country.

Elections for the president are held every six years. Venezuela's president serves as the leader for the country. The president oversees the military and policy with other countries.

Fact!

Venezuela has had 23 constitutions since gaining independence from Spain in 1821.

The president and members of the National Assembly take the oath of office during a meeting of the National Congress.

The courts in Venezuela make sure laws are followed. The country's highest court is called the Supreme Tribunal of Justice. It is located in the Venezuelan capital of Caracas.

What kind of housing does Venezuela have?

Many Venezuelans in cities live in high-rise apartment buildings. These apartments are replacing traditional Spanish-style houses. But traditional homes are still common in rural areas.

Where do people in Venezuela live?

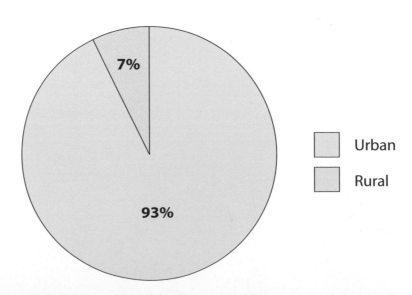

7%

93%

Urban

Rural

Today, high-rise buildings make up most of the city skyline of Caracas.

Since the 1940s, many Venezuelans have moved from the country to cities looking for jobs. The poorest people live in homes made from cardboard and metal. They have no water or electricity.

What are Venezuela's forms of transportation?

Venezuela's government has spent much time and money building roads. Most of the country's paved roads are in the north. Throughout the country, paved and unpaved roads are used to transport people and goods.

Although roads are important, few people own a car. Most people have to go to work on buses or on the subway.

Fact!

Large ships from the ocean can travel on Venezuela's Orinoco River for up to 248 miles (400 kilometers) to cities like Tucupita.

Nearly a million people in Caracas travel on underground trains every day.

Venezuela has more than road transportation. There are over 1,000 rivers in Venezuela. People use boats to transport goods on the rivers. There are over 300 airports in Venezuela that people use for air transportation.

What are Venezuela's major industries?

Most people in Venezuela work in service industries, such as education and health care. Tourism is one of Venezuela's most important service industries. People from around the world enjoy Venezuela's tropical climate and landforms.

Many Venezuelans work for **petroleum** companies. Petroleum made Venezuela one of the richest countries in South America.

What does Venezuela import and export?	
Imports	**Exports**
manufactured products	petroleum
other foods	fruits & seafood
machinery	mining products

Sardine fishing is important to the economy of Venezuela.

Venezuela has other natural resources. Iron, coal, and gold are mined in Venezuela. Fishing is a growing industry. Fishers catch more than 500,000 tons (453,592 metric tons) of fish each year.

What is school like in Venezuela?

School is free to all students in Venezuela. Children must go to school from ages 6 to 15. They learn reading, math, and writing.

After the age of 15, some students go to a secondary school. They study many subjects, including science and **technology**. Some prepare for college.

Fact!

Venezuela has one of the highest literacy rates in the world. At least 93 percent of Venezuela's citizens know how to read and write.

Venezuelan students attend secondary school.

Not all Venezuelan children finish secondary school. Many children of poor families only go to school through the age of 15. They usually leave school to find jobs and earn money to help their families.

What are Venezuela's favorite sports and games?

Baseball is the most popular sport in Venezuela. Many towns have teams that play in large stadiums from October to February. Some Venezuelan baseball players come to the United States to play on major league teams. Ozzie Guillén played on four major league teams and became the manager of the Chicago White Sox.

Venezuelans also play soccer. In Venezuela, soccer is called *fútbol*.

Fact!

The Spanish introduced bullfighting to Venezuela. It remains a popular spectator sport today.

Venezuelan baseball players celebrate after winning a Caribbean Series baseball game in Valencia.

With 1,750 miles (2,816 kilometers) of coastline, Venezuelans take part in many different water sports. Some favorites are swimming, fishing, and water skiing. Sports fishing contests are popular along the northern coast.

What are the traditional art forms in Venezuela?

Venezuela is known for its artists. Native Indians produced art before Columbus came to Venezuela. Later, Spanish-style religious paintings and sculptures followed. In the 1900s, modern art began in Venezuela. Kinetic art became popular. Artists who use the kinetic art form create art that looks like it is moving. Jesús-Rafael Soto was famous for his kinetic sculptures.

Fact!

Romulo Gallegos is one of Venezuela's most famous writers. He also served as president in 1948.

The small size of the cuatro makes it easy to hold and strum.

Music and dancing are popular in Venezuela. Venezuelans enjoy music from **maracas** and four-stringed guitars called *cuatros*. The national dance of Venezuela is the *joropo*. It is a fast, lively dance for couples.

What holidays do people in Venezuela celebrate?

Venezuelans celebrate many Roman Catholic holidays. One of the biggest celebrations of the year is Carnival, usually held in February. It is held 42 days before Easter to mark the beginning of the **Lenten** season. Some towns also celebrate Corpus Christi, which is in May or June. People put on devil costumes to scare away the devil.

What other holidays do people in Venezuela celebrate?

New Year's Day
Epiphany
May Day
Battle of Carabobo Day
Discovery of America

During a Corpus Christi celebration, devil dancers hold maracas and sticks and dance in the streets.

Venezuela's liberation from Spain is celebrated on July 5 as Independence Day. The man who led the fight for independence is also celebrated. Parades mark Simón Bolívar's birthday on July 24th.

What are the traditional foods of Venezuela?

Venezuelan food is influenced by the native Indians of Venezuela. People eat an Indian bread called *arepa* with most meals. An *arepa* can also be stuffed with anything. Most often, cooks fill the bread with eggs, cheese, or meat.

Fact!

Venezuelans celebrate Christmas with a special holiday food called hallaca. *This corn meal pie stuffed with meats and raisins is wrapped in the leaves of a plantain and boiled.*

Venezuelans can buy arepas *and* empanadas *at an* areperas, *or food stand.*

The largest meal in Venezuela is eaten in the afternoon. It may consist of any variety of fish, shellfish, or meats. Beans, rice, and *arepas* are usually served with most meals.

What is family life like in Venezuela?

Families in Venezuela are very close. Often, children, parents, grandparents, aunts, uncles, and cousins live in the same home or nearby. Families help take care of young children while the parents work.

What are the ethnic backgrounds of people in Venezuela?

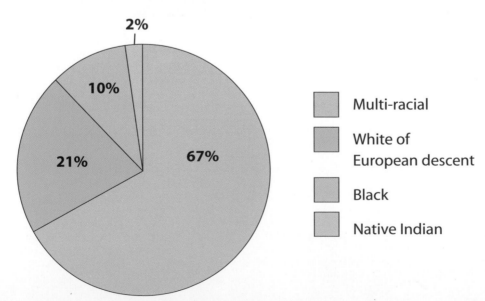

2%

10%

21%

67%

Multi-racial

White of European descent

Black

Native Indian

A family goes holiday shopping together in Caracas.

Sunday is the traditional day for Venezuelan families to go out together. For this reason, museums, parks, and restaurants usually have special attractions such as clowns and live music.

Venezuela Fast Facts

Official name:

Bolivarian Republic of Venezuela

Land area:

548,080 square miles
(882,050 square kilometers)

Average annual precipitation (Caracas):

32 inches (about 81 centimeters)

Average January temperature (Caracas):

70 degrees Fahrenheit
(21 degrees Celsius)

Average July temperature (Caracas):

74 degrees Fahrenheit
(23 degrees Celsius)

Population:

25,375,281 people

Capital city:

Caracas

Languages:

Spanish, about 30 native
Indian languages

Natural resources:

petroleum, coal, diamonds,
gold, natural gas

Religions:

Roman Catholic	70%
Protestant	29%
Other	1%

Money and Flag

Money:

Venezuela's money is the bolívar. In 2006, 1 U.S. dollar equaled 2,147 bolívares. One Canadian dollar equaled 1,845 bolívares.

Flag:

The Venezuelan flag has three equal stripes of yellow, blue, and red. A coat of arms is located on the left side of the yellow stripe. The blue stripe has an arc of seven five-pointed white stars. These stars represent the seven provinces that supported independence in 1811.

Learn to Speak Spanish

Spanish is the official language of Venezuela. Learn some Spanish words.

English	Spanish	Pronunciation
hi	hola	(OH-la)
hello or good-bye	buenos dias	(BWAY-nohs DEE-ahs)
yes	sí	(SEE)
no	no	(NOH)
please	por favor	(POR fah-VOR)
thank you	gracias	(GRAH-see-us)
you're welcome	de nada	(DE NAH-dah)
good	bueno	(BWAY-noh)
name	nombre	(NOHM-breh)
good-night	buenas noches	(BWAY-nas NOH-chess)

Glossary

democracy (di-MOK-ruh-SEE)—a form of government in which people choose their leaders

dictator (DIK-tay-tur)—someone who has complete control of a country, often ruling it unjustly

Lenten (LENT-en)—relating to the 40-day period before Easter, in the Christian church's year

maraca (ma-RA-ka)—a musical instrument that looks like a rattle

petroleum (puh-TROH-lee-uhm)—an oily liquid found below the earth's surface used to make gasoline, heating oil, and many other products

protest (pro-TEST)—to object to something strongly and publicly

technology (tek-NOL-uh-jee)—use of science and engineering to do practical things

Internet Sites

FactHound offers a safe, fun way to find Internet sites related to this book. All of the sites on FactHound have been researched by our staff.

Here's how:
1. Visit *www.facthound.com*
2. Choose your grade level.
3. Type in this book ID **073686413X** for age-appropriate sites. You may also browse subjects by clicking on letters, or by clicking on pictures and words.
4. Click on the **Fetch It** button.

FactHound will fetch the best sites for you!

Read More

Aalgaard, Wendy. *Venezuela in Pictures.* Visual Geography Series. Minneapolis: Lerner, 2005.

Conley, Kate. *Venezuela.* The Countries. Edina, Minn.: Abdo, 2004.

Jones, Helga. *Venezuela.* A Ticket To. Minneapolis: Carolrhoda Books, 2000.

Index